How to Get Your Ex Back

Reliable Research And Expert Guidance On How To Win Back Your Ex And Regain Their Affection, Even If They Are In A Committed Relationship

(Regain Your Former Companion, A Manual On How To Fall Back In Love With Your Ex, A Relationship Of Your Dreams, And Techniques For Acquiring Any Woman Or Man)

Howard Larochelle

TABLE OF CONTENT

The Advantages Of Separating Yourself From Your Ex-Girlfriend 1

How To Adhere To The No Contact Policy 6

The Radio Silence Theory: Severing Contact To Foster Regeneration 21

How To Determine Whether A Partnership Is Worth Keeping 37

How Should You Handle Your Partern's Other Woman? 55

Why Did The Relationship End? 68

Identify The Cause Of The Breakup 82

How Hormones Can Spoil A Perfect Relationship ..99

The Advantages Of Separating Yourself From Your Ex-Girlfriend

It permits you both to recover. You both must take some time to process the end of the relationship after splitting up. This entails permitting yourself to experience both happy and sad feelings. To avoid feeling judged or under pressure, distance yourself and your ex-girlfriend.

It allows you time to consider the partnership. It's simple to become mired in the details of a relationship and lose sight of the greater picture. By giving yourself room, you can take a step back and examine the connection with objectivity.

This can assist you in determining your mutual strengths and limitations as a pair and what kind of relationship you are looking for.

It conveys to your ex-girlfriend your regard for her. You can express your respect for your ex-girlfriend's feelings, and her need for privacy by giving her space. This is significant because it demonstrates your maturity and consideration for others her.

Giving your ex-girlfriend space is critical if you truly want her back. Although it's not always simple, doing this is the best thing you can do for her and yourself.

Additional Advice

Don't discuss her with your loved ones or friends. This will simply make you miss her more and make it harder for you to forget about her.

● Avoid evaluating yourself against other men who she might be seeing.

This is a formula for disaster. It's critical to remember your individuality and why your ex-girlfriend was with you.

● Avoid attempting to arouse her envy. This is a deceptive strategy that will probably backfire. Rather, concentrate on bettering your life and yourself.

● Have patience. It could require some time for your ex-girlfriend to express her desire to reunite with you. Don't immediately give up on her.

These pointers will put you in a good position to win your ex-girlfriend back.

Examine Your Relationship

After you and your ex-girlfriend have had some time to yourself, it's time to examine the relationship. This is a crucial stage since it will assist you in determining what went wrong and what you can do better the next time.

Take into account these actions:

● List your partnership's advantages and disadvantages in writing. What skills did you possess? What tasks did you need to complete?

● Consider the reasons behind your disagreements or altercations. What set you off? What set her off?

● Think about the way you communicate. Was it successful? Were there any areas in which your communication could have been improved?

● Determine your requirements and goals. How could your ex-girlfriend fulfil your needs? Why did she require your help?

● Consider your objectives and ideals. Do they align with the principles and objectives of your former partner?

After you've examined your relationship, you'll know more about what went wrong and what you can do to make things right the next time. This information will be useful if you wish to get your ex-girlfriend back.

Advantages

● It aids in problem identification. To solve an issue, you must first identify it. By examining your relationship, you can pinpoint the precise issues that led to its breakdown.

It facilitates the creation of plans. Once you know them, you can begin creating a plan to address the issues. Adjusting your expectations, communication style, or self may be part of this plan.

- It conveys your sincerity to your former partner. Your ex-girlfriend is more likely to think you're serious about getting back together if you can demonstrate that you've taken the time to assess your relationship and create a strategy to make it better.

To win your ex-girlfriend back, it's crucial to evaluate your relationship. Though it's not always simple, the effort pays off.

How To Adhere To The No Contact Policy

Anything that functions correctly must adhere to guidelines to produce the intended results. Regarding the No Contact Rule, many guidelines are available to assist you. The fundamental ones, which are essentially the foundation of all other rules you may encounter online or in any book about this rule, will be the ones you cover. To make the rules easy for you to comprehend and eventually follow, I will try to keep them as straightforward as possible.

A partnership must always abide by a set of rules to thrive. Rules are put in place to promote harmony and peace within a group or organization. If you adhere to these guidelines exactly, you may have a chance to make things right after you split up with your lover.

The following guidelines can be helpful to you during your No Contact period:

I. Asking: Do You Fit Under the No Contact Rule?

Not everyone is eligible for the program; for example, you cannot follow the rigorous No Contact Rule if you live, work, or attend school with your ex-spouse and have children together. This is because conversing is typical in the specified environments.

You must occasionally have genuine conversations with your ex to ensure your child is doing well. Even during the No Contact time, you cannot cut off communication with the father of your kid; instead, you must implement a more flexible version of the regulation.

As you converse, be sure that you never stray from the three boundaries and start talking about relationships, whether it be about a child, a working relationship, or school. Since you both seem mature, you can cohabitate with your ex-boyfriend without feeling uncomfortable.

II. Enter No Contact When Things Get Tough

If your partner breaks up with you, go into the No Contact Rule immediately. Making an effort to talk your partner into staying with you after a breakup is the worst thing you can do. You may lose your only opportunity to reconcile with your ex if you continue to beg, as it portrays you as dependent and clinging.

It's common for people to strive to mend a broken relationship because they are emotional beings. You must never let him feel satisfied when you cry after he breaks up. When a guy breaks up with you, and you don't cry, he will wonder what happened, and nothing is better than leaving him in suspense. He will start chasing you, but don't break the rule before the period ends; just keep him going.

III. Ignorance Is Acceptable

This is a chance for you to take a deep breath, take stock of your life, and concentrate on your passions and long-term goals. Remember that for the No Contact Rule to be effective, you must genuinely have no contact with your ex. You may begin the rule full of enthusiasm, but eventually, your curiosity may get better.

It takes very little time to pay for a relationship you truly want to succeed—a month or two is enough. Making sure you don't engage in any personal conversation during this time demonstrates your strength and ability to support yourself without a man's assistance.

When you successfully navigate through this time, you emerge victorious and guilt-free. It's not important whether you get him back; what counts most is who you will become after this phase ends.

IV. Removing Their Influence from Your Life

"Out of sight, out of mind" is commonly used to refer to friends or relatives who have passed away, usually without any specific context. This is a really powerful way to move on from someone. Just get rid of everything that makes you think of your ex, including his pictures, Facebook, and other social media accounts. You should also block him and erase his phone number to avoid being tempted to answer his calls because they won't go through. Gather all the sentimental items he has left you and place them in a box you will later take somewhere you cannot easily reach.

This step is important because it demonstrates your strength as a woman if you can convince yourself to let go of things that have brought you joy and conceal them till the phase is gone.

Being a person who stands up for what you believe in is appealing to both men and women. In an emergency, especially if you and your ex have children together, you can lose the phone number, but keep a paper copy on hand.

V. Keep Busy, i.e., get on with your life. It is not advisable to wait for the No Contact period to end while you sit around in grief. This is a serious error that needs to be avoided at all costs. You should use this time to validate your worth and show that you can survive without him.

Keeping occupied is a certain method to reduce your time thinking about your ex. It can be difficult to keep him out of your mind when you are just at home doing nothing because your mind is blank, and you might fall for that incorrectly.

Enjoy a fun-filled evening with your pals; while you're at it, you could even engage in some rebound sex. Rebound sex is a great medicine to help you begin the healing process of moving on from your ex. You can't pursue a reconciliation with your ex if you are constantly dwelling on him; you will never succeed in your quest for his return. Remember that habits are worse than diseases; while you can treat a condition with medication, breaking a habit will require time and effort.

Where Did It Go Wrong in Chapter 1?

Determining the reason for the breakup is one of the first stages towards mending the relationship. Pay attention to the key limitations that may have led to conflicts in the previous partnership. The focus should be on identifying the most frequent reasons for disagreements. Determining the primary reason for the breakup can increase the likelihood of a happy life if the partnership is restored.

You ought to be able to identify the root cause of the issue and devise plans to never deal with it again without fear or favour.

As a preventative step going forward, it is also preferable to concentrate on the general reasons for separation after identifying the primary cause of the relationship's breakup. People's subconscious mind must alert them when anything that appears negative is about to happen. As a result, you'll be able to conquer the difficulties that lie ahead.

Recognizing the Common Reasons for Divorce to Prevent It in the Future

Typically, miscommunication, infidelity, or a lack of trust between the partners are the main causes of separation. It is essential to recognize each other's shortcomings to assist one another in a good relationship. Thus, effective communication is the only way to do this.

Separation also stems primarily from mistrust. When a couple loses faith in one another, distaste grows, and problems become harder to resolve. If allowed to grow, it eventually becomes the main cause of misbehaviour, disrespect, jealousy, and unfaithfulness. The likelihood of a relationship ending increases significantly when infidelity or cheating occurs. Consequently, lies gradually start to surface in an attempt to justify unfaithful behaviour. Right now, the partnership is unstable. The loving gesture fades, and assigning blame is the following incident.

Chapter 2: Is Their Return Really What You Want?

Let's face it: it's difficult and problematic when a relationship ends. It's never easy for individuals devoted to a relationship to break up, regardless of the reasons behind it. It has the power to completely change their reality. People are even more deeply upset by it because it represents the end of a partnership, shared goals, and promises. A relationship ends when there's a lot of suffering, significant disappointment, rage, and grief. A recovery guide can be a great resource for people.

You may be experiencing loneliness right now. Maybe you've believed there's no good reason for you to exist. Without your special someone at your side, you feel unworthy and are plagued by questions about the whys and what-ifs of your broken relationship. You're terrified of the unknowns that await you.

Closure and accepting reality are two of the most crucial steps people must take. You would not benefit from continuing to speak with your ex frequently. Make sure to make up your mind, meet with your ex-partner for the final time, and express gratitude for the times you shared.

Most people allow the mistakes they believe they made in the relationship to hurt them. When you experience this, it's necessary to take stock of your actions and realize that, while you may have made mistakes, it should never be used to justify treating yourself like a total failure. Rather, take what you've learned from those errors and recognize your strengths. Work on them; never let anyone or any unpleasant event pull you down.

Seek ways to avoid the ghosts of your past if you're still experiencing haunting feelings from them. You will succeed with confidence in yourself, even though it might not be easy. However, avoid using drugs, alcohol, or anything else that can be harmful to your health.

Besides, be among trustworthy people who have optimistic perspectives in life. Try to express your feelings whenever possible, but try not to think too much about your feelings for your ex. Instead, try to enjoy talking about some other topics that are important to you. Spending time with family, friends, and support groups would be a great idea.

In addition, you can pursue a previous goal that you have always had. Learn new skills and become an expert in cooking, painting, dancing, and other areas. As a result, this is the greatest moment to be creative and transform negative energies into positive ones.

It's never simple to move on from the baggage of a previous relationship. You can always rely on our list of relationship breakup tips, and never forget that you can take control of your life and break free from the pain. It takes time to heal, so you shouldn't consider dating again until you're positive you're ready. Remember that you have a long list of wonderful things ahead of you. Never pass up the chance to take advantage of these chances and improve yourself!

Chapter 2: Work on improving yourself

When someone breaks up with their partner, they blame the other person rather than take responsibility for their actions. To be a good leader, you must accept full responsibility for your actions and focus on improving yourself rather than your former partner. Not only can improving yourself help you win your ex back, but it will also make you a more complete person. Seeing someone improve and evolve is one of the most alluring things. And yet another of the worst things to witness is when someone deteriorates, and nothing is done about it.

The airline stewardess advises passengers to put on their oxygen masks before helping others in the event of an emergency landing. I think the same applies to how you should live your life. If you do not take care of yourself first, you will be attractive to no one. I believe that for certain people, this is occasionally the beginning of the issue. After they get together, they begin to prioritize everyone else before themselves. Don't get me wrong, some of the world's wealthiest individuals are also among the most generous. However, I think there's a thin line between being a little self-centred and prioritizing your needs so that you have more to offer others.

Advice on improving yourself

What is it that you've been meaning to start but haven't been able to for the longest? Some people habitually let go of themselves when they enter a relationship. Everyone else is taken care of, but not themselves. It's time to put yourself first and be selfish since you'll have more to offer the world if you do this.

Have you been considering going skydiving or going to the gym to get in shape? It's time to quit putting things off; I'm not sure what it is that you need to get done. Go out and pursue the goals you've had in mind. Your ex will be shocked to learn that you are pursuing your aspirations and objectives because they have likely listened to you talk about them for the longest time. You don't need to call your ex to let them know what you are up to in today's society. Post photos of your activities and how wonderful life is going if you use social media. Because you broke up with them, your ex is probably expecting you to be moping around and depressed. When they discover you have been spotted on social media, how do you think they will react?

Go indulge yourself.

After reading this book, set up an appointment to go and pamper yourself; if you prefer going to the spa or doing similar things, take a vacation and have fun. Changing environments and taking some alone time can occasionally aid in improving decision-making. Thinking clearly will allow you to view your situation from a different angle. It would also provide you with an opportunity to mentally refresh yourself if you will.

You've undoubtedly noticed that I don't spend much time discussing what your ex did wrong throughout this book. "I thought this book was going to be about me getting my ex back?" is presumably what's on your mind. You're right—the book is about winning your ex back. However, as I've already mentioned, you are the most important aspect of this situation. People focus on things that are beyond their control far too frequently. This can be a very trying circumstance. From now on, only devote attention to the things you can control; what you know you can control is yourself.

The Radio Silence Theory: Severing Contact To Foster Regeneration

Now, let's discuss a method that has been employed for centuries by individuals to deal with emotional breakups: radio silence. This idea may seem strange initially, but it has shown to be quite successful.

You did read correctly. Silence. Not a message, Not a single call. Not a single call. Nothing. However, how on earth does breaking off contact aid in regeneration? Isn't communication one of the cornerstones of any relationship, especially in the healing stage?

Herein lays the secret to radio silence's power. I will give you a chance to consider this: How many times have you spoken about something you subsequently regretted in the heat of the moment? How many times have hurtful or irrational remarks made just made things worse?

We've all probably seen this at some point, and that's rather common. Because we are human, our judgment is frequently tainted by our emotions. However, what if there was a method to stop this loop of irrational emotional reactions? What if we could master emotional regulation and engage in more deliberate, mindful communication?

Welcome to the wonderful realm of radio silence.

Simply put, radio silence is the act of withdrawing from communication to emotionally recharge. But don't misunderstand—this is not the time to flee your issues or withdraw from society. Conversely, it presents a chance to confront your feelings and focus on your development.

Several writers and subject matter experts have thoroughly examined the psychology behind radio silence. Dr. John Gottman, the author of "The Relationship Cure" (2001), is one of them, and he emphasizes the importance of quiet time in minimizing conflict escalation and promoting understanding between people.

But, my dear reader, how does it impact you? How can you practice the radio-quiet principle so you can heal properly? What advantages do you anticipate from this strategy?

I'll take you on a voyage of discovery in the upcoming episodes as we examine the function and significance of radio silence in your healing process. I swear it will be an intriguing trip, full of discoveries and surprises.

But allow me to ask you this before we go into the specifics: What is your opinion about silence? Is it peaceful or uncomfortable for you? Have you ever intentionally sought to handle uncomfortable emotions or resolve disagreements through silence?

You might feel many emotions, including curiosity, uncertainty, and dread. That's alright, too. We are, after all, going to be venturing into unknown terrain. But remember that the path to a full recovery is convoluted, paved with unexpected turns and bumps. So grab hold of your feelings and join me as we explore the radio-quiet together.

Let me start by reassuring you that you are not the only one experiencing doubt. Many people have looked at radio silence with worry and suspicion before you. After all, we've been brainwashed to believe that quiet indicates a lack of interest or connection. However, what if I told you that quiet can effectively improve your emotional regulation and self-awareness?

Dr. Ty Tashiro, a personal relationship specialist and the author of "The Science of Happily Ever After" (2014), suggests that radio silence might provide a valuable opportunity to step back, evaluate our emotions, and make healthier judgments. And this, my friend, is the very essence of healthy rehabilitation.

I'll draw you a picture for you. Let's say you and your ex got into a fight just now. You're feeling quite emotional right now and want to text or phone her for comfort or closure. Do you recognize this?

Imagine you choose to take some time for yourself rather than act impulsively. You put your phone away and spend time doing fun, relaxing activities. Maybe you walk, read a book, or just sit and meditate. You take charge of your emotions and don't let them dictate how you behave. That's the power of radio silence, my dear reader.

But what if, amid your radio silence, your ex gets in touch with you? Here's when self-control and dedication to a healthy recovery pay off. There may be a great desire to reply, particularly if you still harbour deep affection for your former partner. But keep in mind that radio silence gives your ex a chance to think back on his or her sentiments and behaviour in addition to serving as a tactic for regulating your emotions.

Dr. Theresa E. DiDonato, a social psychology professor and the author of "The Tipping Point" (2000), contends that distance and space can be useful in assisting people in objectively viewing events. This is particularly useful in love relationships, as intense feelings tend to impair our judgment.

Therefore, radio silence can be a potent kind of communication in and of itself, even though it may appear paradoxical. It makes it evident that you are in charge of your feelings and are dedicated to getting well.

However, how can you put radio silence into practice in your life, and how can you withstand the need to break the quiet when you're feeling particularly sensitive? I hope this section of the book helps you find the answers to these essential and legitimate issues.

First and foremost, it's critical to realize that radio silence is neither a punishment nor a way to control your ex's feelings. Rather, it's a means of allowing yourself the time and room to recover and mature. Your radio silent period can be as short as a few weeks or as long as many months; there is no defined duration. What matters most is that you make your decision and make good use of this time.

One may wonder what precisely it means to use this time constructively. Now, let's examine an illustration. Let's take John, a thirty-year-old man who just went through a trying breakup. Rather than bombarding his former partner with texts and phone calls, John becomes radio silent. He takes up painting again at this period, which he had abandoned when they were dating. During this time, he also makes new acquaintances and gets in touch with old ones. John notices he is becoming more content with his circumstances and himself with time. The real power of radio silence lies in this.

Furthermore, you might experience many feelings during your quiet time. It is useful to remember the statements made by psychologist and author of "Emotional Agility" (2016), Dr. Susan David, who contends that acknowledging and examining our feelings is preferable to repressing or ignoring them. Thus, embrace your feelings, give them space, and let them be. This is an important step in the right direction of your healing.

A journal is something that some people find useful to keep throughout their radio silence. Put your sentiments, ideas, and aspirations for the future in writing. This might be a helpful tool to see how you're progressing over time and to process your feelings.

It's normal to occasionally feel inclined to break radio silence. You may be missing your ex or feel lonely. During those moments, I encourage you to revisit this chapter and reaffirm your decision to follow this route. Never forget that you are doing this for yourself—for your development and recovery.

As you can see, the radio silence route may be extremely rewarding and challenging. Ultimately, this quiet time is about reestablishing contact with the most significant person in your life: yourself. It's not only about stopping communication. And you're coming closer to your objective of a full recovery with every day that goes by. Are you prepared to give it a go now?

By this point, hopefully, you and I agree that radio silence is, first and foremost, an act of self-care and self-love. Even though it could initially seem unsettling, this quiet provides priceless room for emotional recovery and personal development.

Recall John, our painter who rose from the ashes of a strained marriage and illustrates how this quiet can lead to personal growth. In the middle of the chaos, he found solace in that picture, those people he had rediscovered, and that time spent by himself.

Remember what Dr Susan David said when she said that feelings are not barriers to understanding and self-awareness but avenues towards it. Let me restate her remarks so you can carry them on your travels: "Emotions are data, not directives".

This chapter has taken us a long way, sweet reader. We have examined the idea of radio silence, dissected it, and shown its real intent. By doing this, I think it's become evident that radio-quiet is a useful instrument for your healing rather than a cheap trick.

You know, I'm excited for you. I'm excited because I know you'll embark on a life-altering adventure of self-discovery. Imagine having a fresh feeling of purpose, a deeper awareness of who you are, and a distinct idea of your future every morning when you get up. You can benefit from the quiet radio in that way.

However, my dear friend, our trip is far from ending. It's only getting started. The proverb "Rome wasn't built in a day" may come to mind. That also applies to getting over a breakup. In the upcoming chapter, we'll get into the art of personal reconstruction, or, as I like to refer to it, "how to create the best version of yourself." This is the meat of the issue, the basis for all we have discussed. Are you prepared to advance to the following phase of your rehabilitation process? You won't want to miss this adventure, I assure you. Shall we travel together?

Section I

What the No Contact Rule Is and How It Is Effective

Let's now discuss why the No Contact procedure is effective. When most girls break up, what do they usually do first? They devise every possible strategy in an attempt to talk to their man. They phone and text him, see if he's online in the unlikely event that he hasn't missed your calls or texts, and suffocate them with their emotions in different ways. Ladies take note: guys typically struggle to control their emotions when they are overwhelmed! That was not how they were programmed. Furthermore, what do you know? That is not inherently flawed.

A confident, strong man who knows what he wants out of life and appreciates pairing with a lady to spend time with is extremely lovely. Similarly, a strong, independent woman who doesn't crumble into a pile of wadded-up tissues every time she deals with her emotions appeals to men greatly. They simply don't want to see it since, generally speaking, they lack the necessary filter to digest it, so we might do it nevertheless. What we may regard as over-explaining just looks like grovelling to them.

And, let's be honest with ourselves, grovelling does occur!

Thus, this process's "why" is straightforward. We will create a plan to move your life forward rather than you losing it and collapsing into a heap for too long. It's been claimed that waiting is inevitable and that our identity is shaped by how we wait. So, while this is all happening, let's strive to be the finest versions of ourselves, shall we? We will, in turn, provide him with some much-needed space to reevaluate your initial intentions for him. To your great advantage, he will probably take this time to quietly reminisce about all of the wonderful moments you spent together. This wouldn't be the case if you were bugging him constantly.

Rather, he would be recalling how oppressive you are. We will not be going there. Gaining control over the remainder of your life while allowing him the room to do the same is our new "why," We'll be acting from a position of stability and control instead of getting in touch with your ex-partner.

You know the "why" behind everything we'll be doing in this book, but don't worry—I'll be at your side for a while. Now is the moment to commit to yourself. Can you utilize this rule the way it is supposed to be applied? I'm here to tell you that the entire plan will backfire if you go two days without communicating with him and then give in and start texting, chatting, or going to all your old hangouts. It won't work, and you'll appear to be trying too hard. This is a procedure that requires time. And just like any new healthy eating plan or exercise program, there will be challenges. It could even be challenging for a whole week. But isn't that the main reason most individuals employ personal trainers? Since they give up when things get too difficult on their own.

Make sure that's not you! I'm here to support you every step of the way, and you CAN overcome this.

So, right now, write the phrase NO CONTACT on a few Post-it notes. Put a positive statement about yourself underneath each post-it note, such as "I'm worth it," "I'm doing this for me," "This is a good thing," or "I deserve to be happy." Place these in visible locations throughout your home. One should be placed in your car, where you'll see it every day, and one should be on the bathroom mirror. To ensure they always see the message, I've even met folks who tape them behind their phone and then practice setting it to face down. This way, your positive affirmation will already be ingrained in your mind, and you won't be as tempted to text him back when that familiar "ding" alert lets you know you have a message.

Now that we know the rationale behind our approach let's discuss it in more detail. Because you deserve it, girl!

How To Determine Whether A Partnership Is Worth Keeping

Give yourself time to think things through before launching a full-blown campaign to win your ex back. Consider carefully. Is it worthwhile to fight for the relationship?

Is winning your ex's back truly what you want? Or are you just feeling uneasy and alone? Is your only fear that you won't participate in the activities that couples do?

Don't battle for a relationship that will probably end badly again. If the other person is merely going to make you sad again, it is best to call it quits.

You'll need to put in much time, effort, sacrifice, emotional energy, and commitment to get your ex back. Does your partner deserve all of these?

The following advice will strongly advise you to defend your former partner.

It's always fun to spend time with you.

Whatever you two do together is irrelevant. Are you and he engaged in purposeful, fruitful, thrilling, or enjoyable activities? Or are you just lounging about having a good time? It is valuable if the two of you are enjoying yourself just by being together.

You have a list of favourite persons that includes your ex.

Is your former partner your best friend? If he were no longer your boyfriend, would you still look forward to seeing him? If you respond in the affirmative, it demonstrates that you respect your ex-person. This is encouraging for a partnership.

You feel excited by him.

Do you feel obligated to hug your ex and kiss? Or does the mere thought of him make you sultry and agitated? It's encouraging if you find yourself drawn to your ex on a physical level.

You discover a wealth of topics to discuss.

A connection requires communication. The length of time you have been in a relationship is irrelevant. You mustn't grow too accustomed to your spouse that you run out of topics to discuss. Talking to your partner about your ambitions, dreams, and seemingly insignificant daily occurrences should still excite you.

You two are sincere with one another.

A trustworthy and sincere relationship is in good health. You shouldn't feel compelled to read the other person's texts or emails. Both you and your partner should be honest with one another.

You can overcome your obstacles constructively.

Every relationship will experience difficult moments. How do you handle each other in these situations? Do you frequently have passionate and senseless outbursts? Or do you both tend to approach issues maturely and productively?

You're not attracted to anyone else powerfully or profoundly.

Are you drawn to someone else strongly? Is your desire to date him so intense that you can't help but think about dating him? Is your former partner more than simply a fling with another woman? It could be wise to permanently break up with your ex if this is the case.

You have no desire to "pretend" with your former partner.

Do you have to act as though you enjoy a particular music, activity, or film genre? It's not a good idea to act differently from who you are in the hopes that your partner will love you more. A relationship is strong when both partners are at ease with who they are.

Together, you wish to aim for the same objectives.

Do you intend to stay with your partner? Is he observing you in his? Do you share any aspirations and objectives? Are you both willing to discuss and make concessions if your goals differ? The relationship is considered healthy and devoted when both couples envision a future together.

Compare your current relationship to the ideal one. Is it even close? You ought to be persuaded that trying to win your ex back is worthwhile in terms of time, energy, sacrifice, preparation, and strategy. If you share this conviction, you should investigate the possibility of winning your ex back.

Modifying Your Approach and Attitude

Here's the point: you will never succeed if you keep doing the same thing! This is a difficult lesson since it requires you to acknowledge your shortcomings. This is not to imply that you are to blame for the split. Remember that it takes two to make a relationship work and two to end one. But there's probably something you wish you could change, and now is your chance to make that happen.

You must first focus on YOU to win your ex back. This entails altering your perspective on them and how you approach the possibility of ever getting back together. You must break the cycle if you are pining for them and running after them. Not only does this mean that the same event will happen again, but it also leaves you exposed. It's time to concentrate on what you genuinely want to happen here. You have to give your ex the benefit of the doubt if you want them back.

Instead of making this about them, try focusing on yourself.

Give up believing that you depend on them; you don't, and holding onto this belief will hinder your progress. Get outside to take in a little bit of the scenery. For once, take care of yourself and enjoy yourself!

You are putting them out of your thoughts as you focus on yourself and transform into a more positive and productive personality. You are far more inclined to give in and allow them to take the lead when approaching you, which they will inevitably do. You may need to comfort yourself and talk yourself through this entire process. "I'm fine without her," "I don't need him," or any other mantra that will support you will do.

Increasing your self-assurance, altering your perspective, and being aware of what you must concentrate on are the keys to this. Make every effort to set your ex aside for the time being. Even though it may seem illogical, concentrating solely on yourself is the only long-term strategy to win them back. Modify your mindset and seize this chance to assume the desired role. Regaining them will help you; when you do, the relationship will function much better. Consider this a chance; you'll be thrilled if it brings your former partner back!

Proceed with your life and let them witness this.

You likely become angry when someone advises you to move on. You probably ignore people who tell you there are better options or other fish in the sea.

In actuality, you have the exceptional chance to move on with your life by not speaking with your ex for a month. You will discover that, despite your deep desire for their return, you don't NEED them for every breath you breathe.

The No Contact Rule ensures you have time to move on and discover other sources of enjoyment. It demonstrates that life is about more than one individual, and you can even come across old acquaintances or your former way of living. Move on for yourself, not for your ex. There's a distinction because this isn't something you're doing just to piss your ex off. For once, you're doing this for your happiness.

You get to start enjoying yourself and finding happiness outside of this one individual. Eventually, you realize that they are not the centre of your universe and that you can go on and lead a life without them.

Observe what transpires when you utilize this capacity. They become aware! They view the photos you upload to your website, displaying your amazing activities. They observe that you genuinely appear comfortable or cheerful and that your life is going on without them. They are not amused by this at all! You prove that you can move on and that there is more to life than just one person.

You are no longer desperate for them and their attention, but if you can win them back, that is an amazing bonus. When your ex notices your newfound independence, they become more determined to defend you.

They want to have a role in your life and to be the source of your happiness. When they see you moving on, they become much more motivated to put in the effort to get you back, even if they aren't aware that this ignites anything in them. Functions flawlessly and reveals some wonderful facets of your life!

Give them the reins for a change.

You're accustomed to the No Contact Rule, and even if it's challenging at first, you soon realize its advantages. Gradually, you notice that your former partner is emerging from the shadows. It's beginning to seem like a chance to start anew after what seemed like an eternity-long layoff. You're finding that you're ready and able for your ex to take the lead, not that you don't miss them or want them back.

Your ex may have access to your Instagram photos of your amazing adventures. Mutual pals might let them know that you're doing alright. They are secretly obsessed with this!

Most likely, they are also missing you, but more than anything, they want to know how you plan on moving on without them. They experience emotions from this that they were unaware they possessed. They want to return to your life immediately and see what this newfound happiness or confidence is all about!

Your former partner will suddenly start contacting you, which you probably won't believe. Even if they are using a cheap justification, they might give you a call, send you a text, or find another way to communicate. Suddenly, it seems like they have to see you, talk to you, or somehow get back into your routine. When you realize how effective the No Contact Rule is, you may be taken aback. After a difficult breakup, you might not think your ex may reach out to you again, but it can happen, and the outcome will be fantastic!

Your former partner will initiate conversation since they find you interesting and you don't.

You have agreed to the No Contact Rule, and as the allotted time runs out, you will notice that they can no longer assist themselves. They must witness firsthand how content you are. They want you back, and they are going to make the effort.

They will come after you and even try to speak with you in person. You'll understand now that everything worked, and you had a chance to get your ex back by being uncontactable for a month. It feels so good to have something come to you without requiring any effort on your part!

Step 1: Steer clear of these deadly mistakes to stop neediness, insecurity, and desperation from ruining your chances.

This section is labelled "The Instincts" because people make these mistakes because they follow their instincts.

The majority of the advice in this book contradicts common logic, but it is effective.

After reading it, you'll understand why, and everything will make sense.

So, let's talk about the deadly mistakes you should never make first.

Deadly Mistake #1: Constantly Calling and Texting Them.

This is the narrative told by most people who wish to be reunited with their ex-boyfriend or ex-girlfriend. It's a serious mistake to keep getting texts and calls from your ex. It is a grave mistake to give them even a single call.

However, it is not how things work in practice. Every time you message or communicate with your ex, you are persuading them that you are a needy person who would suffer without them. Your neediness separates you from your ex and makes you seem unattractive.

Your intuition tricks you into thinking this is how you'll interact with your ex.

You should always be extra cautious when you go out to drink. You can find yourself embarrassing yourself by phoning your former partner. Consequently, anytime you go out to drink, bring a companion along so they can stop you from doing this.

But how can we get back together if I don't text or call my ex?

Rekindling their sentiments of desire towards you would be a suitable method of contacting them. I'll go into more depth on how to accomplish this later.

Deadly Mistake #2: Pity-seeking and Begging.

If asking for attention after a breakup was effective, no one would ever end a relationship with someone. They decided to part ways with you and obey your cries for help.

Your plea won't change the reason for the split, whatever it may have been. The last thing you want is to come across as weak and insecure, which is what begging will do.

Likewise, your gut will tell you that all you have to do to win your ex back is show them how miserable you are without them—or how reliant on them—or else they will return to you.

Your perspective shifts to something similar.

He'll come back if he knows how sad I am without him.

I can win him back if he realizes his importance to my life.

Again, you're being duped by your intuition.

Nobody goes back to an ex out of sympathy, I promise you. Nobody is attracted to miserable people.

Even if your ex returns, do you want them to be with you out of sympathy?

Or do you want their respect and affection?

According to a professional study, most people choose a secure spouse over an unstable one.

Anything that gives the impression of unease will just turn your ex away, so sit back and think about it. Seeking, messaging them constantly, and overall projecting a sense of desperation are signs of insecurity that will neither pique your ex's interest nor encourage them to pursue a relationship with you.

Deadly Mistake #3: Allowing Them To Trample All Over You.

Your intuition will tell you that if you do all your ex asks of you, they'll return. Your instincts will tell you there is no purpose to your desires, ideals, aspirations, and goals.

Your instincts will tell you that the most important thing is to get your ex back. And you're prepared to sacrifice everything for it.

You gave up on your ex's dominance. You turn into a doormat. You accede to your ex's most ridiculous demands. But something tells you that's okay since the most important thing in life is that your ex is still in it.

But what do you know?

You won't get your ex back by taking him at his word. It will simply make your ex less fond of you.

How can they appreciate you if you don't respect yourself?

Nobody wants to hang around with someone they don't respect. Even if they do come back, they'll go as soon as they see you don't regard them as a person.

Experts say that limits are an essential part of every good relationship. And if you don't have boundaries or respect for yourself in your relationship, you'll probably wind up unhealthy.

Even if you succeed in acting like a doormat to win your ex back, the relationship will ultimately end due to dysfunction.

Deadly Error #4: Loving Them Wholeheartedly

Your intuition tells you that once they realize how much you appreciate and care for them, your ex will come back. Just persuade them that you are the only one who could love them more than anybody else.

How could they possibly reject you once they realize how much you love them?

In actuality, they already know how much you care about them, how much you admire them, and how much you affectionately care for them. Nevertheless, they decided to separate. Their reasons for ending the relationship won't disappear because you love them. You can't make someone change their mind by showing them affection.

The more you smother them, the more imprisoned they will feel. As a result, they will simply get more eager to get away from you as soon as possible.

How Should You Handle Your Partern's Other Woman?

Once a woman marries, she never thinks her husband will leave her, and they will eventually become friends.

However, women are extremely sensitive, and some of them are incapable of resisting the urge to become intimate and personal with a woman other than their wife.

This is an unfortunate reality of today's world, but it's something that spouses need to be able to deal with to ensure that their marriages endure for as long as possible.

It can be quite difficult for widows to maintain their faithfulness to their marriage. While some women are strong and loyal to their gender, others are more likely to easily identify with other women, especially regarding their relationships with them and their motivations.

Sometimes, this may go unnoticed by the women, but ultimately, no secrecy is kept secret for an extended period.

When you, the wife, are friends with your partner's girlfriend, avoiding getting too close to that person is often a good idea. Even though you are friends, there are times when you are unaware of each other's true intentions.

They might be pretentious, so if you suspect this person has feelings for you, you should watch her out and keep your distance.

Furthermore, never reveal to this woman any personal or derogatory information about your relationship or your husband in particular.

Don't divulge too much information because all you're doing is offering her advice on how to catch your man when things go wrong.

You might be worried about giving her a bad impression of your spouse on your part, but in reality, you're supporting her in taking the necessary steps to make her closer to you.

Another thing you may do is show the other woman how much you value their friendship. This is if you have been close friends for a lengthy period. A crucial action you may take in this situation is to express to your friend your desire to live life to the fullest and maintain a lifetime relationship with your family.

It would also be beneficial to reassure her that you would never give up on loving your husband and children and will never allow anyone to get in the way of your marriage.

Some women are incredibly persistent, even though they know the woman they desire is already married and has children. They don't give a damn about harming friends or other individuals.

Therefore, if you know that your spouse is a faithful man, then the best advice you can give him is to not give your partner any reason to leave your relationship. This is especially important for women who have a suspicion that their partners are cheating on them or engaging in some other type of personal relationship. And never give up if you do love your family and your husband.

The Ideal Method for Handling the Loss of Commitment in a Man

Most women aspire to live healthy relationships and spend their entire lives with the person of their dreams. The best feeling in the world is to fall in love with a man, feel emotionally attached to him, and decide to spend the rest of your life with him.

The worst part of being in a relationship is when a man loves you, but he's not ready to commit to you past the initial stages of the relationship.

This situation would not only make you angry but also frustrated. This chapter will be helpful to you because it will help you understand why he feels the way he does and what the ways are that you may influence his thoughts.

The first and most important thing a woman should do is ask him to be married to stop him from insulting her. These women are not prepared for marriage and are not willing to commit at all. If you continue to bother him about the relationship, the situation will worsen, and the relationship will eventually fall apart.

The best thing to do is stop thinking about anything and maintain the relationship as it is.

Women who are afraid to commit have the fundamental fear that they will lose their freedom. They usually believe they will not be allowed to leave with their friends after the marriage.

Since their carer will also suffer, they prefer not to be committed. The best way to deal with such a man is to give him complete freedom. Let him go out with his friends and it will be much better if you encourage him to do so.

The other thing you must do is assist him with his carer. Lead him, be his helpful hand, and always provide support. This will help him feel comfortable and alter his perception of a committed relationship.

Women should keep in mind that just nagging a man to get married will undoubtedly hurt him, and he will cease like you. He will make an effort to live independently of you.

Therefore, the best thing to do if you want to win a man's heart and spend the rest of your life with him is to give him his freedom, which will undoubtedly positively impact him.

You can leave with your friends; that way, you'll have a calm mind. Remember that a man is much more likely to give her one when relaxed and does not have to worry about controlling his spouse. He will also be more likely to give her one if his partner does not press him for a committed relationship.

Examining Your Partnership

Why do you still want to see your ex when you know who you are now and have possibly even attracted attention from new people?

You must be brutally honest with yourself and have a compelling reason for wanting to return.

I am aware that there may be a few reasons why you might wish to return:

You still adore them.

Without them, you could not survive.

You are miserable apart from them; you were meant to be together.

These are still the same motivations you had initially. I need you to dig deeper and determine why you want your ex back.

Before declaring that you wish to see your ex again, you must consider a few things.

The Things You Need to Think About Before Returning

You probably had a lot of questions when you split up with your ex, but the hardest one to answer today is whether you should try the relationship again. Even if it means you will experience heartbreak again, are you willing to take the risk? If the answer is yes, there are a few things you need to consider.

What caused your breakup?

Breakups can have a variety of reasons. If you believe that things are not working out for the two of you and that you are not a good match, it could be abuse, an affair, or incompatibility. Now that you know why you broke up, you must consider whether you can move on from the situation because it will undoubtedly come up again.

What makes you want to return?

What is your reason for returning? Ask yourself. Are your friends and relatives forcing you to do this, or is it for the kids? Is it because you find it difficult to start over with someone else, or can't you handle the financial load? You truly need a compelling argument to declare that you are returning.

Examine the relationship as a whole.

Don't limit your attention to the split. Examine everything, even the events that transpired months before your parting ways. Were things so terrible that you two split up over petty disagreements so you might have a reason to depart? Since they will return, did the two of you address and acknowledge the problem?

Is the problem ongoing?

Did you end your relationship because you were tired of resolving the same issue repeatedly? Certain aspects are psychological and have been there since we were young. The question then becomes, are you prepared to work through this ongoing problem with your ex and support them in finding a solution?

Are you prepared to forgive someone insincerely?

Though you're going back, you have to be able to overlook all of your errors. Since you know this is your ex's weak point, you shouldn't be bringing it up. You must let it go and focus on other pressing issues.

Try making friends before jumping in; proceed with caution!

The only way to be close to your ex and see if they have changed is to take action like this. You are not back together just because you had fantastic sex; you should do this without letting your hormones rule you.

Follow through on the actions.

Though it is simple to let words get in the way of one's deeds, actions always reveal a person's genuine intentions. You should suspect something is wrong if they swear they won't drink and hang out with buddies who do.

You should think carefully before returning to your former partner if you are considering doing so. How do you approach them now that you know what to weigh?

Chapter 1: How to Approach Your Ex-Girlfriend Again for Another Date

You have decided it was not as wise as you once believed to draw the line with your ex-girlfriend. I'm sure you've noticed by now some of the most obvious indicators that she wants you back too—for example, she keeps in touch too frequently, runs into you, inquires about your love life, and so on. You get the idea. However, you don't have to get into it immediately simply because you want to give each other another chance. The wisest course of action would be to consider it briefly before acting rashly.

You'll find some starting points and tips in this post to help you make a good impression on your ex-girlfriend when you try dating her again.

1. Allow enough time to reconsider whatever you can about your past relationship. Reevaluate your position. In your previous relationship, who was the main troublemaker—you or her? Take some time to

talk about it together if she was causing the trouble. If, however, the issue is internal to you, make every attempt to identify the mistake and avoid it in the future.

2. Consider how recently you have shown her special attention. Perhaps she simply wanted you to hold hands while you walked together, and you thought it was absurd, or perhaps she just wanted flowers now and then. Try to be Mr. Spontaneous occasionally by surprising her with small gestures like romantic notes expressing your love for her or by delivering flowers to her place of employment. Remember, the devil is in the details.

3. Request a date with her. A romantic date with your ex-girlfriend will reignite the flame between you by bringing back happy memories, and memories also evoke happy, past sentiments. After the evening, you two could as well reignite old passions, so make an effort to look as exquisite as you can.

4. Let her know that you want to get well. Show her that you've changed as a guy by being willing to discuss and engage in activities you've never dared to do before. Express interest in her interests, or start a new pastime together that will lead to lots of cuddling.

5. Ask her parents for permission to court her to gain their sympathies in front of her. In this manner, you'll make her feel incredibly unique and look more romantic.

Here are five quick and uncomplicated steps you can take to start dating your ex-girlfriend again. Just remember never to rush anything. You will quickly win her back if you just try to be a patient, kind guy who is genuinely interested in her interests and has an open mind.

Why Did The Relationship End?

Using cause and effect is one of the most popular approaches to issue-solving.

Goodbye is not an exception. Finding out what kind of issue you have is always the greatest place to start, no matter what issue you face. If a relationship ends, you should first determine what caused it.

Writing it down could be a smart idea for future use.

Things to take into account when figuring out why a relationship ended

This subheading may sound like the heading of a thesis section, but that's a good thing. Even if it can be painful to analyse a lost relationship, you must find a method to move on from the situation. If you want to reunite with your ex-lover permanently, consider the bigger picture and take responsibility for your faults.

Sincerity

This is a crucial component in figuring out why the relationship ended. Being impartial and truthful about the topic becomes challenging when emotions run strong, and you are too close to it. Remember that you don't have to assign blame just because you understand why you and your partner split up. That is just untrue. Deciding who was at fault is not the point. Instead, you should consider how you could improve the next time and be truthful about the cause of your breakup. A tango involves two people. Naturally, the issue of what partners can do to strengthen their relationship arises. Communicate openly about the part your partner will play, but remember to stay upbeat once more.

For instance:

Correct Response: To express your concern for your relationship, you would spend more time with them.

False: You won't have as much time to spend with your partner.

Both may mean the same thing, but things may appear more promising for you and your ex based on how you interpret your objectives and plans. Of course, your ex is subject to the same guidelines.

The right response is that your partner will be more sensitive to your emotions. Untrue: Your significant other won't treat you badly.

To put it plainly, you are both discreet and honest. Try to read between the lines and refrain from saying harsh things to each other when discussing and considering the cause behind the breakup.

Finish

Splits do not always occur due to decisions made by both parties. There are moments when it's entirely biased. You must first achieve closure if you're trapped after a breakup and don't know what to do. Hopefully, your former partner will be amenable to mediating a resolution. If not, there are two actions you can take. You could also attempt to ascertain the cause of the split on your own. You might also just ignore it. It's better to avoid drawing unfavourable conclusions about your former partner. That's not a smart place to start if that's the settlement you're searching for.

IS IT WORTH THE EFFORT, AND WHY DO I WANT TO GET BACK WITH MY EX?

Even years after the breakup, receiving notification from your former partner may cause you to fantasise about getting back together or, at the very least, to experience some degree of wistfulness. For various reasons, you haven't grieved the connection yet, even though you genuinely feel something for this person.

Even though so many wonderful memories remind you of your time together, it can't be love, and you genuinely don't want to regret anything.

If you believe you are the only person who has ever experienced this, don't act absurdly. A significant portion of the quite large group of people I tutor who separated some time ago share your sentiments! Because of all their memories, many people feel the urge to be with their ex again.

How, then, can you explain that some people can move on quickly while you cannot get your ex as far away from you as possible?

There are undoubtedly a lot of explanations for why, despite the partition, you truly need to be close to them. Although your warm feelings are certainly not unwelcome, they are typically not the intended outcome.

It's important to remember that this is not an easy situation because you have so many questions, and you're not sure if trying to get back together with your ex is wise.

Deciding to try to get back together after a lengthy separation is not easy; therefore, you need to share the reasons behind your desire so you can figure out the best approach later.

"Willis Gottman, for what reason would I like to get back with my ex after the amount they hurt me?" is a question I am regularly asked. It's anything but an easy question to react to because every relationship is incredibly novel.

Because of this, I advise reading "How to Get Your Ex Back" or scheduling a training session so that you can benefit from personalised guidance.

Eventually, you should be aware that I could identify the five most common reasons we observe in people because of my background as a teacher and mentor.

Why would I want to reconcile with my former partner? Identify two "great" reasons why!

No, if you're thinking about your ex months or even years after the breakup, it doesn't mean they've left you with some kind of grudge! I'll explain a few things about this oddity, which will probably have something to do with your current situation.

You probably think it's terrific that you want your ex back since you're still in love with them or because you regret making a decision that was made too quickly. If you end up in the next class, be sure you're not experiencing severe dependency or exalting your former partner.

The Essential Justification: I adore my former partner and find it impossible to imagine my life without them.

Although I have briefly discussed the main reason you would want your ex back at the beginning of this book, I haven't gone into great detail about it.

It has to do with love! Though it is the most delicate since it is unstable, it is typically expected to be the most logical explanation when you think it is the primary factor guiding you. There are a lot of little clarifications, but because your emotions are taking over, you've been confused and cannot recognise other factors.

This doesn't mean you're not feeling loved; it suggests that you probably feel a sense of domestic dependency. This is not entirely bad, though, because all you need to do is reestablish equilibrium.

You're thinking, "I truly love my ex," and you're regretting the misunderstandings that caused the breakup. It's very usual to start over and make changes to a solid relationship so that you may make sure you regret nothing and are happy.

You now realise how important they are to you and that this is the perfect opportunity to show them the best version of yourself! (Clearly, sensibly speaking.)

I regret being parted!

Here, we're talking about folks who decided to depart rather than those who bid farewell for good. But eventually, they realised that their ex was The One. If you also find yourself in this situation, you can undoubtedly relax since, if you decide to part ways, you can always get back in the saddle!

Considering everything, you should never allow regret to rule your life because it can potentially ruin it. A person might think they would be happier and have the opportunity to have a better relationship with someone else. Still, if you are mourning the loss of the person you were sharing your life with before, you won't have the choice to move forward with something else.

You'll come to regret that decision as well.

There is additionally the responsibility. You're second-guessing your decision to split up today because you hurt someone. Occasionally, you want things to exist for them to become conspicuously clear.

Chapter 1: Getting your ex back

If you and your significant other recently ended things, don't assume that everything is lost and that you have lost your relationship forever. Getting your ex back is far easier than you would think, and you can still do it.

You may have noticed that things aren't progressing as you had hoped, even after trying to communicate your wish for reconciliation with your ex. If it seems like your ex has forgotten about you, what should you do?

You most likely want your ex back, just like most people do. Most of the time, it's far simpler to say than to do. If your ex says he or she no longer loves you, can you win their heart back? Unfortunately, very few of us know how to win back your ex's affection after they've gone on. You can, however, employ some strategies to raise your chances of earning their love and getting them back.

Two people come together to develop a relationship. Ultimately, however, the people you have commonalities with could impact your relationship with your spouse. Don't expect that to alter once the relationship ends. Among the many factors you will need to consider to get your ex back are people close to you and your ex.

Using mutuals is one of the easiest strategies to win your ex back. This doesn't mean you have to approach them and try to convince them to assist you in getting your ex back. It might work, but the odds are slim, and your ex might think it's inappropriate. It would also appear that your friends are taking sides and putting them in a difficult situation.

Continue to hang out and accompany them to events. You must maintain strong relations with your mutual friends to regain your ex.

They could even impact the breakdown or continuation of your relationship once you have successfully gotten your ex back. Stop pestering them about your former partner. Avoid coming across as obnoxious.

Furthermore, stay out of your ex's face as much as possible. After a break, this will enable you to keep a certain level of intimacy with your former partner. While attending events together, keep your relationship with your ex informal for now. Following a breakup, it will be incorrect to avoid your mutuals.

Another common misconception about problems in relationships and reconciliations is one's gender. Being a guy or a girl won't make it any easier to reconcile with your ex. Understanding the benefits of your gender can even increase your chances of reconciliation, but that is a discussion for a different time.

"Why have I been hearing about all the difficulties with reconciliation so far?" may be on your mind if you're feeling down. There's a reason behind this madness, so don't worry. It's only meant to give the impression that getting back together with your ex won't be all that simple.

But there is still hope! Your chances of getting your ex back are 100%. This book is one of the most crucial pieces of advice.

You may have been instructed to listen to your heart, and you may already be doing so if you want the person you love to return and be by your side and in your life once more. Though it is excellent advice, there are other things you should consider doing as well. In the end, you have to see reconciliation as the objective.

The next thing you need is a strategy after you have a goal. It's necessary to plan, weigh the advantages and disadvantages, and carefully consider your options. Understanding your mistakes, how to get your ex back, and when to do it is also critical.

Put another way, maintaining a happy and productive mindset is as important as getting your ex back. If you continue to be stubborn and conceited about what you should and shouldn't do to get over your ex, this book won't help you. You have to respect the advice of the professionals and be aware of it. Nothing or no one can aid you unless you actively seek help and are open to receiving it.

Before starting this trip, ask yourself these three important questions.

Do you still have feelings for your ex?

Are you willing to remain receptive to suggestions about what to say and do to get your ex back?

Do you believe in yourself and your ability to get your ex back?

You have the greatest chance of getting your ex back if you can say "yes" to each of the queries above.

Identify The Cause Of The Breakup

Do you recall the classic fairy tales where the handsome prince weds his lovely princess and leads a happy life together?

Their main flaw is these stories' inability to show us the outcome of the characters' marriages. This leads us to conclude that being in a relationship is a sufficient cause for loving life and possibly being the happiest person alive.

But in actuality, everything is influenced by external factors.

Your relationship may eventually take a positive turn or take a negative turn.

In certain broken relationships, both parties frequently blame the other for various offences. The fact that neither of them will back down makes everything more difficult. Every human has an ego, and they can become overbearing during stressful situations like a breakup.

The least you can rely on during a breakup is your ego. Rather, make an effort to evaluate both your relationship and yourself. Try to identify your shortcomings and draw a connection between them and the current circumstance. How did you get to this position?

We can then move on to comprehending the causes from here. They now exist in various forms. While some justifications are within the limitations of hyperbole, others may be rational.

Going over each one will make you one step closer to moving past the breakup and getting back together with your partner.

Bad behaviours are a major reason why many relationships fail. Perhaps your spouse is a compulsive gambler, or perhaps you smoke habitually and avoid criticism.

In any case, habits can damage relationships because they are annoying or cause health problems. We can all agree that excessive gambling or smoking might be bad. However, some of us will stubbornly stick to these routines even in the face of breakup threats. It's possible that your partner has been overly worried about you, and they think that ending the relationship is the greatest option for forcing you to give up your habit. However, it doesn't seem to be the most efficient.

Interaction

Everyone can agree that communication can help any relationship grow, but it may also be the first step towards a failed one.

Relationships are simple at first. Here, communication is not too difficult to do. However, you'll probably run into a few roadblocks if you allow yourself enough time.

Things become complicated when one of you tries to bring out the worst in the other. And the root of this is the ongoing argument over trivial matters.

Arguments over words are normal. However, if things continue unchecked, you will eventually reach a point where you can no longer bear it.

Individual Space

One of the many fundamental components of a relationship is cooperation. You would need to address each other's issues and meet each other's needs for it to work. However, there will come a time when you will take things too far and start controlling the other.

Too much power sometimes works against your partner's interests, creating even more issues. The best action in these situations is to allow each other the personal space they require. When this is denied, one will feel constrained and will split up.

What Didn't Go Right

If you want to preserve any hope of reconciling with your ex, it's critical to comprehend what went wrong. This entails identifying the precise cause of the breakdown in your relationship.

You may begin making the necessary corrections once you clearly know what went wrong.

Living with someone who is the other sex, has a different educational background, and might not always accept your behaviours is not always easy. A relationship is more than feelings; it's about two different worlds trying to come together. To find out why your relationship ended, you must comprehend what went wrong.

It's therefore expected that you will make mistakes. However, how can you correct or defend your errors? How can you explain the situation if your spouse doesn't agree and you think your acts were appropriate? What types of mistakes lead to relationship breakups?

It's important to strike a balance between your expectations and your tastes. This section will teach you how to recognise these errors, steer clear of them going forward, and provide an apology when needed.

Insufficient communication

varying degrees of dedication

One individual believes they are aware of their partner's thoughts and emotions.

One individual doesn't feel valued

Unresolved hostility or bitterness

money issues

Adultery

When one begins to change, the other finds it difficult to accept it.

Violence or abuse

misuse of substances

Below is a more detailed explanation of each of these arguments. Don't worry if any of these problems are occurring in your relationship now! I will give you a few ideas that might work to address them. You must first determine where things went wrong to avoid repeating the same mistakes.

One of the primary causes of relationship breakdowns is a lack of communication. Couples that don't talk to each other live in two different universes. Little issues quickly grow into major ones because everyone sees things differently. This frequently results in mistrust and hatred.

Solution: Having an honest conversation with your spouse in person is the best method to handle this situation. Ask them directly instead of attempting to decipher their thoughts or read their minds! By doing this, any future misconceptions will be avoided. Additionally, confirm that you understand exactly what you expect from the partnership. It's critical to have an early conversation if one party has desires that the other does not.

Varying degrees of dedication A significant cause of friction can arise when one person is prepared for a committed relationship while the other wishes to take things slowly. This might happen when one feels that they are giving the relationship their all while the other isn't contributing at all. This frequently leaves one individual feeling bitter and undervalued.

The best action in this situation is to talk to someone about your expectations. If there is a discrepancy, it is crucial to determine the reason. Perhaps one individual desires children while the other does not. Or is it possible that one individual desires marriage while the other does not? If you want the relationship to succeed, you must know these aspects. It's better to call it quits before things get too convoluted if you can't agree on these basic points. It shouldn't take a whole person's life to provide happiness to another.

One believes they are aware of their partner's thoughts and emotions: This is a prevalent issue frequently resulting in miscommunications and animosity. One is effectively treading water when one begins to assume things about one's companion. These presumptions quickly develop into grudges, and the relationship begins to fail.

If you are guilty of this, the best course of action is to apologise. Admit to your partner that your assumptions were incorrect and promise not to make the same mistakes twice. Additionally, be more honest and open with your relationship by sharing your feelings and views. Doing this can improve their knowledge of you and avoid future misunderstandings.

One individual doesn't feel valued: This is a typical relationship issue. People begin to feel unimportant and ignored when they believe they aren't being recognised. This frequently results in mistrust and hatred.

The best action in this situation is to express gratitude to your partner. Tell them why you adore them and what they mean to you. Remind them often rather than just once! Additionally, give them a loving message, prepare their favourite dish, or get them flowers as small gestures to make them feel loved. Your partner will undoubtedly feel valued in return if you try to express your appreciation for them.

Unresolved hostility or grudges: One of the main things that destroy relationships is this. It is impossible to address anger and resentment when they can linger for too long. Both parties will eventually give up and end the relationship.

The best action is to confront your partner directly if you harbour any resentment or hatred against them. Discuss your concerns with them and attempt to reach a solution. Seek expert assistance if you're unable to complete this on your own. Admitting that you need assistance to resolve a problem is not a sign of weakness; it demonstrates your willingness to go above and beyond to keep your connection together.

Monetary issues: A partnership may experience significant stress when finances are tight. One person can begin to feel like they are the only one working, and the other is not contributing. This frequently results in arguments and hatred.

The best way to handle this situation is to gather together and draft a budget. Determine and maintain the amount of money you need each month to pay for your expenses. Assist an individual who habitually exceeds their budget in controlling their expenditures. Find inventive ways to earn extra money; you may sell some of your possessions or take up odd jobs. The relationship will be considerably less stressful when both parties cooperate to achieve a shared objective.

Infidelity: While it can be challenging to overcome, it is not unachievable. Forgiving someone who has cheated on you is the best thing you can do. Simply forgive them and move on; don't try to explain or justify their actions. You can mend the connection with time and patience, but it won't be simple.

The best course of action, if you were the one deceived, is to face your spouse. Discuss with them the events that led up to their dishonesty. Try to resolve the problem jointly by being open and truthful with one another. Seek expert assistance if you're unable to complete this on your own. Couples counsellors are highly qualified professionals who can assist you in resolving your problems.

Who Else Wouldn't Want to Meet New Friends Easily?

Adapting to a new community may cause trouble making new friends. You have a passing familiarity with everyone. You experience loneliness.

Is it enough to simply sit there and wait for someone to approach you, extend a hand, and ask you to be their friend?

I doubt it. You've got to make the move.

How to?

1. Examine yourself

Decide the kind of individuals you want as friends initially. Do you want to be friends with others who share your interests and hobbies, your gender, or your age? Or would you prefer to be friends with people who pull at entirely different heartstrings so that you can discover goods in life that are more interesting in other ways?

2. Avoid shyness!

I am aware that it might not be simple for certain folks. But you wouldn't be able to make friends easily if you continued to be a shy person. As I previously stated, take action. Fortitude, letting go of any fear in your heart, and approaching someone you think you have a certain comity with

3. Put on a happy expression.

Not a boo but a real and lovely smile. Those like those with wide smiles over those with panting faces.

4. Be authentic

Don't pretend to be anything. But you must be wary of being someone else, not the real you, so you won't find it interesting to keep the connection going. Should you choose to?

5. Avoid becoming crazy to fail

Expecting to make a true buddy on your first try is unrealistic. Prepare yourself for failure. Friendship requires chemistry as well. It's always possible that the person you addressed earlier does not have chemistry with you or that you do not have chemistry with them.

Some take their friends for granted. However, they learn that friendship is like a flower that needs to be watered and fertilised when they find themselves in a circumstance where they have no friends and must make some.

Creating Online Friendships and Social Networks

Everyone wants to socialise and make friends, but they don't know how to accomplish it. This essay will teach you how to expand your social circle more quickly.

Joining an association: By joining associations, you can meet more people. Make sure the organisation you join will benefit you or that you can fit into. You may join a choral group or singing organisation based on your interests, goals, and vocal abilities.

Those who are proficient with an instrument are qualified to join a band. Politics-inclined people can readily approach a social association member where they can make money. It's beneficial to join new organisations where one may develop and make a difference. Additionally, you can make more friends in this way.

Attending parties: You will meet new people if you go out and socialise; if you stay to yourself, you won't meet many.

Like nothing else, partying will bring people together and introduce you to new individuals. Therefore, if you want to create new acquaintances, make sure you get out and attend events of a similar nature. People meet at these gatherings, including sand parties, reunions, and platoon structure exercises. These are the most popular gatherings where you can socialise if nothing else.

Online friends: These social networks are constantly available to make new acquaintances and spread the word to new acquaintances. To find online pals, you may sign up for social networks.

Without a doubt, two of the biggest and most well-known social network websites are Twitter and Facebook. Additionally, some allow you to speak freely with pals you've made online, which is a chic way to make new acquaintances.

These are just a few of the many ways you can meet new people and create a lot of friends. Feel free to try any of them out.

How Hormones Can Spoil A Perfect Relationship

Remember when you were happy and excited to see your partner? You would have been doing things that raised your self-esteem all day.

As a woman, you may have relieved some of your tension by talking to your girlfriends about various issues; this would have raised your oxytocin levels.

Relationships might end up falling apart very rapidly when hormones are high. Hormones can make people impulsive, greedy, and sensitive, which makes it difficult for couples to have healthy communication.

This could lead to miscommunication, arguments, and, ultimately, the dissolution of the partnership. An individual's mood can be altered by hormonal imbalances, leading to impulsive behaviour or excessive emotional outbursts.

This could lead to conflict between the two, making it difficult for them to speak to each other responsibly and reasonably.

Hormonal imbalances can also cause physical issues that impact one partner's appetite or desire for sexual activity, which can strain a relationship.

Any relationship has to be aware of one's hormonal state and how it could affect one's partner to last and succeed.

Needs and respecting any boundaries may need to be set to create a healthy relationship.

If hormones have caused the relationship to deteriorate, it is imperative to try and rebalance it using natural remedies, counselling, and honest communication.

With perseverance and care, a wonderful relationship can be salvaged and even strengthened by understanding the impact of hormones.

It's essential to comprehend how hormones interact if you want to keep your connection strong. Be mindful of your partner's needs and maintain open lines of communication so that everyone feels free to voice their opinions without fear of criticism.

Respecting and understanding each other's needs can help keep the relationship from failing because of hormones. Finally, but just as importantly, it's important to recognise how hormones impact relationships and work together to try and overcome any issues that may arise.

By maintaining a strong bond and honest communication, any couple may overcome the difficulties caused by their changing hormones and continue to enjoy their amazing relationship.

It would have felt amazing!

But after a hard day at work, your ex would have been tense and exhausted. He doesn't want to talk about his problems because talking about them makes the wrong hormone surge in his body.

All he wants to do is relax, and maybe the world's problems can be fixed while he watches TV for a little bit.

However, he now has to deal with a partner who wants to talk, share, and cuddle with him when he's stressed.

Chapter 5: Moving Slowly

As they say, good things come to those who wait. Another moves very slowly but surely. Like many things, getting your ex back is something you shouldn't do quickly to avoid accomplishing the reverse of what you intended.

It's Not Always Better to Go Fast

Rachel sends her ex-boyfriend Chad a brief text message since she misses him. Hello. How are you doing? After a few minutes, to her joy, Chad responds, "Good." You?

Perceiving that Chad is also grieving for her, Rachel writes a long text message expressing her loneliness, her need for him, and her belief that their breakup was a mistake.

After an hour without a response, Rachel texted Chad again to inquire if he had heard her previous message. After thirty minutes with no response, Rachel calls Chad. When making a second effort, Rachel gets the dreaded message, "The subscriber you are calling is currently unavailable," when Chad does not answer.

Chad's phone battery ran out, or he turned it off to prevent Rachel from contacting him.

It's Easy and Slow

After your first text message is answered favourably, keep trying by sending a few brief, inoffensive messages each day or two. Unless your ex is also hatching a plan to win you back, in which case, it is excellent for you to avoid making bold claims of love during your first week of messaging.

You must gradually reintegrate into your ex's life rather than forcing yourself upon them. Expect opposition, especially initially, and don't expect your ex to instantly welcome you back into their life. Keep your cool and avoid being pushy, needy, or clinging when you do. Honour your former partner and the speed at which they are moving. Don't forget to give him or her some privacy as well. You don't want to be overly attached when trying to get back together.

WHEN CONFLICTING RELATIONSHIPS

Unfortunately, even the best relationships can fall from time to time, but there's usually a reason for it, even if we can't always see it at first.

There are several reasons why fulfilling relationships break down and result in divorce. You might have had meaningless arguments or simply found out that your ex stopped talking to you before withdrawing, keeping you in the dark about what was happening.

People who are hurting and unsure of their partner's position in the relationship frequently end up behaving in ways that are entirely at odds with what they should do to win their ex back.

This is done so that women will generally employ tactics that appeal to them, and men will act in ways that make sense to males. It is important to learn that men and women think differently. As is the contrary, i.e., applying feminine logic to get a man back, applying masculine logic to the problem of winning a woman back is sometimes counterproductive.

The terrible thing about this is that, despite their best attempts, both men and women in these situations tend to act in ways that, unknowingly, will repel and push away the person they are trying to get back into their lives.

This suggests that they frequently behave in the opposite way to win back their ex and include them in their life again, even though they are unaware of it. Think about this. Is your current plan of action for getting your ex back effective? Or does it just make you feel worse than you already do by removing you from that person?

Let's examine some of the factors both sexes consider in relationships and how they interpret each other's actions. These insights can frequently lead to a much better understanding of what could have gone wrong in the relationship and what to do when healthy relationships break down.

The biology of men and women differs.

Not only are there physical differences between us, but there are also significant hormonal and other biological variances that set us apart from one another.

For example, did you know that men frequently look for ways to reduce stress by increasing their testosterone levels? They will, therefore, watch the news when they get home to learn how to begin their own "fix it" mentality after a difficult day. Because it motivates them to do so, people may find it rewarding to resolve the problems of others. That might be what he's thinking about, even if he might be sitting motionless on the couch. While controlling his stress, he won't be able to assist with problems in the real world.

They will feel much better about the world when their testosterone levels are up and only try to address their problems after they have calmed down sufficiently, especially after a long day at work when they spent the day trying to prove to their loved ones how fantastic of a provider they can be.

Regrettably, women's biological drives differ fundamentally from men's, which can cause problems in relationships. For example, a woman who has higher levels of testosterone in her body may have more tension and feel the need to dispute with her partner about trivial matters that are unlikely to be understood by them.

Women will figure out how to release the stress-relieving hormone oxytocin. Ironically, oxytocin is acknowledged in non-scientific.

In addition to being the bonding hormone that pushes a woman to develop stronger ties with her partner, it is also called the "cuddle hormone". It has a strong association with maternal behaviour.

Today, for women to release oxytocin, they must feel appreciated, loved, and cherished. When they perceive their partner is withdrawing from them, for whatever reason, their stress levels increase, and they may become defensive, rather than the hormone testosterone flooding their system.

A male experiences a similar reaction when his testosterone levels fall, which is an increase in stress and a protective stance.

Well, that's interesting to hear.

HOW A GOOD RELATIONSHIP CAN BE RUINED BY HORMONES

Remember when you were happy and excited to see your partner? You would have been doing things that raised your self-esteem all day. If you're a woman, you might have talked to your girlfriends about various issues you're facing to decompress, raising your oxytocin levels.

It would have felt amazing!

But when your ex got home after a hard day at work, he was probably stressed and exhausted. He doesn't want to talk about his problems because doing so makes the wrong hormone increase in his body. All he wants to do is unwind and perhaps, for a few hours, while watching TV, all the world's problems will be solved.

But now he has a spouse who wants to talk, share, hug, and show affection at a time when his stress levels are up to an unacceptable degree. After a busy day, he hasn't had time to unwind, and now he has to deal with a partner who doesn't seem to be in too much of a hurry and doesn't seem to care about what he needs. Even though this is a simple example, do you see the problem? Even the best relationships could end if people are unaware of these fundamental hormonal differences between men and women.

Of course, there are additional causes for failed partnerships.